Great Mysteries

HAUNTED HOUSES

by Janet Riehecky
illustrated by Lydia Halverson
with cartoons by Dan Siculan

Created by

THE
CHILD'S
WORLD

Distributed by CHILDRENS PRESS®
Chicago, Illinois

cover illustration by Lydia Halverson
cover design by Kathryn Schoenick

CHILDRENS PRESS HARDCOVER EDITION
ISBN 0-516-06216-6

CHILDRENS PRESS PAPERBACK EDITION
ISBN 0-516-46216-4

Library of Congress Cataloging-in-Publication Data

Riehecky, Janet, 1953-
  Haunted houses / by Janet Riehecky ; illustrated by Lydia
Halverson, cartoons by Dan Siculan.
    p. cm. — (Great mysteries)
  Includes index.
  Summary: Describes supposedly true incidents in which houses have
been haunted, in such categories as "Friendly Ghosts," "Animal
Ghosts," and "Vengeful Ghosts."
  ISBN 0-89565-454-7
  1. Ghosts—Juvenile literature.   2. Poltergeists—Juvenile
literature.   [1. Haunted houses.   2. Ghosts.]   I. Halverson,
Lydia, ill.   II. Siculan, Dan, ill.   III. Title.   IV. Series: Great
mysteries (Elgin, Ill.)
BF1461.R5   1989
133.1'22—dc19   88-38780
                                                           CIP
©1989 The Child's World, Inc.   AC
Elgin, IL

1 2 3 4 5 6 7 8 9 10 11 12 R 97 96 95 94 93 92 91 90 89

Great Mysteries

HAUNTED HOUSES

CONTENTS

Chapter 1

Ghosts in the House

Have you heard footsteps outside your room when nobody was there? Have you heard chains rattle or mysterious moans in the night? Perhaps you've walked through a cold spot in a room and suddenly felt as if someone were watching you. What does all this mean? Well, it could be just your imagination. Or maybe someone is playing a trick on you. Or maybe, just maybe, you are living in a haunted house!

Most people think a house has to be old and creepy to be haunted. Or that some tragedy has to have happened in it. But that's not true. Just about any house can be haunted. Beautiful southern mansions, New York high-rise apartments, and midwestern farmhouses have all seen their share of ghosts—or at least they claim they have.

But why? What is it that attracts ghosts to certain places? Well, sometimes ghosts haunt a place where some great tragedy has occurred, but they haunt for lots of other reasons as well. Sometimes they linger to fulfill some promise or comfort those they left behind. Some ghosts just seem to like to cause mischief, and some want revenge. And then, sometimes, there just doesn't seem to be any reason at all for the haunting.

Sussex, England Haunting

There didn't seem to be any reason at all for a ghost to haunt Rose Morton and her family, but one did—for seven years.

Rose Morton was nineteen years old when she and her family moved into a new house in Sussex, England. The house was large, attractive, and only twenty years old. Rose was a medical student, and all she had on her mind was studying. But then one night she saw a tall, thin woman, dressed in black and holding a handkerchief to her face, glide down the stairs. She didn't look like anyone Rose had ever seen before.

Rose followed the mysterious woman for a short distance, but then her candle went out. Rose returned to her room, wondering who the lady could be. Over the next few months, Rose saw the lady on several occasions. Rose knew the lady must be a ghost, but she was more curious than scared. Being a scientist, she decided to study the situation to see what she could learn.

Rose fastened string across the stairs to see if the lady could pass through (she could). She tried to photograph

the lady (it didn't work). Then she tried to communicate with the ghost (no luck). She knew the lady wasn't just her imagination because six other people in the house also saw her. Guests also sometimes heard footsteps and the rustle of the lady's skirt.

Rose's family tried to find out who the mysterious lady was. They talked to people who knew the previous residents of the house. One of the previous residents fit the lady's description. She was the second wife of a man who had never gotten over the loss of his first wife. He drank heavily, and the two fought constantly—especially over the first wife's jewels. The man finally hid the jewels in a secret compartment under the floor of one of the rooms. One day the wife had had enough and moved out. Shortly after that the man died. His wife died two years later.

Rose and her family couldn't see any reason for the lady to return to a house in which she had been so unhappy. She didn't seem to be looking for the jewels, and she never went into the room with the secret compartment. She never seemed to threaten anyone or to try to get attention. Apparently, she just didn't have anything better to do.

Rose and her family grew accustomed to sharing their house with the lady, but eventually she began to appear less and less often. Her image became vague and blurry. Finally, seven years after her first appearance, the lady ghost disappeared for good—leaving Rose and her family just as confused as they had been when she first appeared.

Beverly Hills Haunting

Rose and her family didn't mind living in a haunted house, but some people do—especially if they have just bought a beautiful new home in Beverly Hills.

Elke Sommer is an international film star. Her husband, Joe Hyams, is a famous journalist. They are the kind of people the President invites over for dinner—not the kind of people you expect to see ghosts.

In July of 1964 Elke and Joe moved into their new home in exclusive Beverly Hills. Things began quietly. A few days after they moved in, a guest saw the figure of a man go into the dining room. When Elke checked, no one was there. Two weeks later, Elke's mother woke up to see a man standing at the foot of her bed. He vanished just before she could scream.

Elke and Joe began hearing noises in the night. Night after night there seemed to be a dinner party going on in the dining room. When Elke left to shoot a film in Yugoslavia, Joe felt there was still someone in the house—especially when windows came unlocked during the night, and he heard the front door open and close, even though he had bolted it tight before going to bed.

Joe placed microphones and tape recorders inside and outside the house. The ones outside never picked up the sound of anyone approaching the house, but the ones inside recorded the familiar sound of chairs moving in the dining room. Each time Joe went downstairs to investigate, all the chairs were in their places and the sounds stopped. But when he went back upstairs, the sounds started again.

Joe joined Elke in Yugoslavia, but strange things continued to happen at the house. They hadn't told anyone about their experiences, but a friend staying at their house told them it was "creepy." He had heard strange noises and the window in his bedroom opened by itself. A private detective, hired to keep an eye on things, found doors standing open a short time after they had been securely locked. Once, all the lights in the house went on at 2:30 in the morning. Moments later they all went off again. The mysterious figure of the man in the dining room was seen by a man who came to clean the swimming pool and by a friend of Joe's who had come to visit for a few days. The friend was so scared, he went to a motel.

Elke and Joe allowed investigators from the American Society for Psychical Research to study their house. A total of thirty-six investigators came. Though they couldn't agree on who was haunting the house, they all agreed that the house was haunted. They tried to contact the ghost to find out why he was there, but they didn't have any luck. One woman thought she had reached him and that he had agreed to leave, but the noises still continued.

Joe and Elke were not happy about having their sleep disturbed all the time, but they finally concluded that they'd just have to learn to live with their ghost. In an article for the July 2, 1966 *Saturday Evening Post*, Joe said that he wouldn't let a living man drive him out of his house, and he didn't intend to let a dead one either. Then on March 13, 1967 a fire suddenly broke out for no apparent reason in the dining room. Elke and Joe escaped safely,

"There isn't any such thing as a ghost!"

but they had had enough. They moved out and put their haunted house up for sale.

No Such Thing?

There are many people who will tell you that there are no such things as ghosts. They will tell you that all a house needs to become haunted is for someone with a lot of imagination to move in. But there are other people who are not so sure. Every culture on earth has reported some sort of ghosts haunting its people. And very ordinary, down-to-earth people have seen things no one can explain.

When people like the Hyams report strange goings on, it's hard to dismiss their stories as just imagination. Police officers, newspaper reporters, doctors, lawyers, and even Presidents have reported seeing or hearing ghosts. These people aren't lying, and they're trained to observe well. Maybe they are mistaken about what they think they've experienced—and maybe they're not.

This book tells of some average (and not so average) people living in ordinary (or extraordinary) houses who think they've seen or heard or smelled or felt a ghost. Every story in this book was told by someone who believed it to be true. You make up your own mind.

Chapter 2

Friendly Ghosts

There are many reports of "friendly" ghosts who haunt the houses of people they love. It doesn't seem to matter whether these ghosts knew the people living in "their" house before they died or not. These gentle spirits like to do good deeds. And it can be really helpful, sometimes, to have a ghost on your side.

A Ghostly Call

One afternoon Gaye Spiegelman was working in the kitchen of her San Francisco home. Her son, who was only a year and a half old, was playing in his room. According to Hans Holzer in *Haunted Hollywood*, Gaye suddenly heard, "Mommy, come quickly" over the house intercom. Gaye rushed upstairs and found her son turning blue. He had swallowed a nickel and was choking.

Quickly Gaye grabbed her son and pounded on his back. The nickel came loose, and her son could breathe again.

The little boy was saved, but a mystery remained. Who called Gaye over the intercom? It couldn't have been the boy. He had a nickel blocking his throat, was too little to work the intercom, and couldn't really even talk yet.

Gaye didn't puzzle long over this mystery. She had been convinced for quite some time that the ghost of her mother or grandmother was living in the house. Missing items had suddenly appeared in places that had already been searched, and Gaye had felt the presence of a warm, caring spirit on many occasions. Now Gaye just smiled and thanked the ghost for saving her son's life.

In Minneapolis, a young man rented a duplex with a resident ghost. The ghost had cared a lot about her house and garden. So, when the young man took special care of the place, the ghost was pleased and decided to take care of the young man. When he was annoyed by some other tenants, the ghost decided to help. Every day while the young man was at work, the ghost made a lot of noise. Soon the other tenants couldn't take it anymore and they decided to leave.

Friendly ghosts can be very helpful. They may tuck children in bed, warn about danger, or help solve problems. The winners of a New York state lottery reported that the ghost that haunted their house annoyed them by making lights flicker and cabinets open and close, but they also thought it brought them lots of good luck—including their 2.5 million dollar win. Friendly ghosts can even be fun to have around.

Beam Me Up, Scotty?

At Kansas State University a haunted fraternity house had a mischievous, but helpful ghost. This ghost turned lights on and off, opened locked doors and windows, and made all kinds of noise. But he also repaired broken clocks, and, during an ice storm in 1973, he did the men of the fraternity an especially big favor. The electricity was out for several days on the whole street, but every day the electricity in the fraternity house came on at exactly 4:00, so everyone could watch their favorite TV show—*Star Trek*!

Delta Sigma Phi fraternity house, Kansas State University (courtesy of Kansas State University; Dan Donnert, campus photographer)

A Ghostly Warning

A California couple told ghosthunter Hans Holzer that their ghost may have saved their lives. Both had been aware of ghostly footsteps and unexplained cold spots in their house, and once "Mrs. H." heard a woman sobbing terribly. Then one night both the husband and the wife saw a ghostly figure in their dreams. The ghost was in their bathroom. It reached out of a bathtub full of water to the light switch. When the ghostly arm touched the switch, sparks flew and the hand withered. When the husband and wife found they had had the same dream, they called an electrician. The electrician said the old light switch was both illegal and dangerous. He confirmed that if someone had reached from the bathtub to the light switch, that person might have been electrocuted. He fixed the switch.

Giving Ghosts

Friendly ghosts will even sometimes bring gifts. These objects that appear out of nowhere are called *apports*. In the 1970's in New York the Ackley family treasured two such gifts. They found silver tongs in their house when their daughter got married and a gold baby ring when their first grandchild was born. They could only explain these gifts in terms of the ghosts they'd seen and heard in their house over a period of nine years.

And in Tennessee in 1817, a ghost known as the Bell Witch brought some gifts when Mrs. Bell became ill. The Bell Witch spent most of her time tormenting the members of the Bell family (see Chapter 6), but she seemed to like Mrs. Bell. When Mrs. Bell became very ill, gifts of nuts and fruits dropped from nowhere into Mrs. Bell's bedroom. And when Mrs. Bell was too weak to crack the nuts, the ghost did it for her.

Visitors to the Bell house tried to figure out where the fruit and nuts came from. They appeared to drop from thin air. No one seemed able to explain them. One day some visitors not only received fruit and nuts, but also heard a voice from the air tell them to "eat and enjoy." Even more mysterious, the gift fruit (oranges, grapes, and bananas) couldn't be found in Tennessee in those days. The ghostly witch explained that she brought them from the West Indies.

The Ghost That Keeps on Giving

And then there are some ghosts who just don't know when to stop.

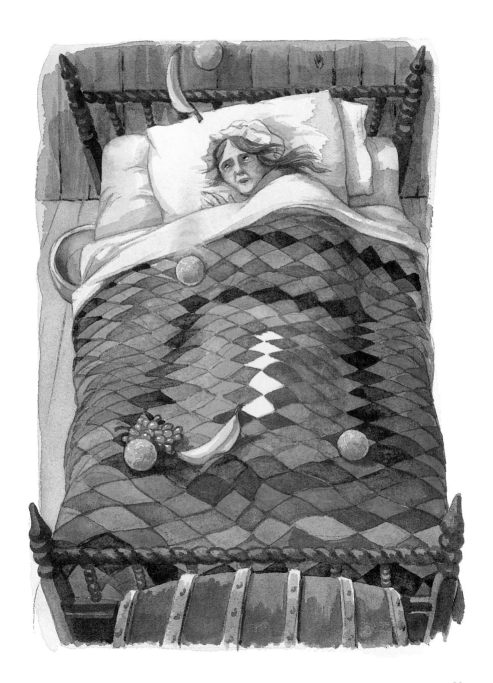

On a small farm in Maine, Marshall and Jessie Creamer lived—for a short time—a happy married life. However, as sometimes happens, after a few years they began to fight. Most often, they fought over the amount of wood Jessie burned in the stove. Marshall had to saw and split the wood, and he got mad about how much Jessie burned up. He put Jessie on a "budget." He would give her a wheelbarrow full of wood each day. When it was gone, she was out of luck.

The two continued to bicker, and eventually Marshall got so angry, he moved out of the house. He ran the farm and Jessie ran the house, and the two never spoke to each other again. However, Marshall always brought Jessie her wheelbarrow full of wood each evening.

Everything went smoothly for a long while. Then Marshall died. Jessie didn't know what she'd do about the

wood. Before she had anything figured out, the problem was solved. Four days after Marshall died, she looked out the window and saw the ghost of her husband chopping wood. The ghost left her the wood at the back door as usual. And for the rest of her life, Jessie received her wheelbarrow full of wood each day.

But then Jessie died. And nobody knew how to tell the ghost. He still kept delivering wood every day. No one lived in the house, so somebody had to make a special trip just to carry in the wood every day. Soon wood was stacked in every room of the house.

Finally, someone bought the house. Knowing a good thing when he saw it, he had it written into the deed that the ghost came with the house. The October, 1969, *Harper's Magazine* reported that several other people lived in the house over the years, but that no matter who

"I just don't know how we ever got along before we got Bessie."

they were, they were presented with a wheelbarrow full of wood each day.

Part of the Family

People who share their houses with friendly ghosts consider their ghosts to be part of the family. Often they have good reason to be grateful they have a ghost around. Skeptics claim that living people account for the good deeds of these ghosts, but those who claim to live with friendly ghosts will never be convinced of that.

Chapter 3

Ghosts with a Mission

Many ghosts have a reason for their haunting. Some are worried about loved ones they left behind. Some wish to right a wrong. Some are trying to fulfill a promise they made while alive. And some want to reveal the truth about how they died. Most of the time, these ghosts stop haunting once they succeed in finishing their task. But sometimes they keep at their task down through the years—and through the pouring rain.

The Rail-yard Ghost

One night during the depression, a hobo got off a train in a small Ohio town. It was raining, and the man shivered with cold. As he looked around, wondering where he could spend the night, a man in a raincoat approached him and offered to let the hobo spend the night at his house.

The hobo gratefully accepted and followed the man to his house. The man told him to go inside, but did not follow him in.

A woman with two children greeted the hobo kindly and fed him a warm dinner. The hobo wondered why the man who had brought him to the house didn't join them. The woman told him that it was her husband who had brought him. Her husband liked to wander the rail yard on stormy nights, she said, and often brought someone home for dinner. She told the hobo that he shouldn't worry about it.

The hobo spent the night in the guest room. He didn't get much sleep, though. Footsteps paced the hallway, and the sound of knocking disturbed his rest.

The woman's son went with the hobo to the rail yard in the morning. As the hobo waited for a train, he talked with the young boy. The boy told him that his father, the man who had invited the hobo to stay, had been killed in a rail-yard accident six years before. The hobo had been invited to visit by a ghost!

Haunting for a Reason

The rail-yard ghost was a ghost with a mission. He watched over his family during the night and helped people who were down on their luck. The hobo he helped that one stormy night didn't leave on the next train. He came back and lived in the guest room of the ghost's widow until he was able to get a job. He helped the family, especially the son, and reformed his life—all because of a ghost with a mission.

Murder Will Out

Maria Marten's ghost was set free once she exposed the man who murdered her.

Maria's family didn't believe her when she claimed that the young man she was dating wanted to marry her. He was from a wealthy family. Maria was from a poor family. They warned Maria that he was lying to her, but Maria wouldn't listen. Then one night Maria ran away. Her family thought that she had run away to get married. Sure enough, a note arrived from the young man. He said he had married Maria and taken her to London to live.

Everything was fine, except that a ghost that looked like Maria began haunting Maria's stepmother. The ghost appeared several times telling the stepmother that the young man hadn't married her—he had murdered her! The ghost told her stepmother to look in a nearby barn. There she would find Maria's body.

At first Maria's stepmother thought she was just imagining the ghost. Finally, though, the family decided to search the barn. They found Maria's body just where the ghost had said it was. The young man was found in London and arrested for murder. Maria's spirit was then able to rest.

A Nun's Quest

Justice was not quite so swift for a nun in Suffolk, England, though. She had to wait more than a hundred years to fulfill her mission.

Year after year, the ghost of an unhappy nun was seen wandering the gardens and house belonging to a church in Suffolk, England. The different ministers who lived in the house and many of their guests all saw her on different occasions. Many people down through the years tried to figure out who she was and what she wanted. She looked so unhappy and seemed to be asking for help. Then, finally, a woman who claimed she had a special ability to communicate with spirits from other worlds was able to talk to the ghost nun. The ghost said that she had been in a convent that had once stood on that spot. A man had taken her from the convent and murdered her. He was long since dead, but she couldn't rest until her bones received a Christian burial. She led them to her bones. The minister buried them properly, and the ghost nun appeared no more.

A proper burial is very important to many ghosts—and they can make it worth your while to help them.

A Ghostly Reward

Back in pioneer days, a young couple spent a night in an abandoned cabin. Before they settled down to sleep, the wife saw a ghost in the main room. It was an old man with a cane. Her husband was outside and didn't see him. In the morning when the husband suggested that the cabin might be a good place to make their home, the wife said, "NO!" She told him that the cabin was haunted, but he just laughed.

As soon as the husband left the wife alone in the cabin, the ghost appeared again. The wife was scared, but the ghost told her not to be. He promised to show her where he had hidden some money and the deed to the house if

she would find his bones and his wife's and bury them properly. They had been murdered by thieves and their bones left in a nearby cave.

The woman dug where the ghost told her to dig and found a pitcher full of money. When her husband came back to the cabin, he didn't laugh anymore. Together they found the bones of the old man and his wife and buried them. They they settled down happily in their no-longer-haunted house.

Ghostly rewards can be great, but beware of ghostly punishments!

Keep Your Promises

In 1875 in France, a dying woman's husband promised her he'd say prayers for her after she died. When he didn't keep his promise, she haunted him. First there were shadows that darted here and there in the house they had shared. Then strange noises disturbed the night. Finally, a fiery ghost appeared, demanding her husband keep his promise. She grabbed his nightcap and left scorched fingerprints on it. This finally got through to the man. He said the prayers, and the ghost left him in peace.

Promises, Promises

Many ghosts are concerned more about the promises that they made while living. One woman reported that her landlord visited her one afternoon. He told her that some workmen would be at her apartment the next morning to fix some holes in her ceiling as he had promised. The woman was pleased—until she learned that her landlord had died of a stroke a few hours *before* his visit. Another woman was surprised to see her father at her front door one afternoon. He had been promising to visit for quite some time, and now he was keeping that promise—a few hours after he died.

And then there was a man who was haunted by the ghost of his first wife. Though he had loved her, the man was scared by her ghost. He worried that she was angry that he had remarried, so he talked to his priest about it. The priest reminded him what a good woman his first wife had been. He suggested that the next time the ghost appeared the man should just ask what she wanted. The man did, and the ghost responded. She had died owing a small sum of money to the butcher. Would he please pay it? The man did, and the woman was able to rest.

Unfinished Work

Sometimes ghosts take on the most important task of all—saving lives. In *Ghosts Around the House*, Susy Smith tells of a strange case which happened in the Cook household, near Salt Lake City, Utah.

At first the Cook household had a typical haunting. There were strange noises in the night and a ghostly touch at unexpected moments. Mrs. Cook learned that a young man had hung himself in the attic and decided that he must be the ghost.

Then the ghost began making occasional appearances. When Mrs. Cook asked him why he didn't go on to the spirit world, the ghost answered, "My work here is not finished."

But the ghost didn't seem to be doing any work as he popped in and out over the next couple years. Then one day in December of 1968, Mrs. Cook went up into the attic to get some Christmas ornaments. She climbed up to the attic through an entrance in the attic floor. The hole for the entrance was where the young man had hung himself. A rope with a loop near the end still hung there. People held onto the loop for balance while getting into a storage area in the wall next to the attic entrance. Mrs. Cook grabbed the rope and stepped up on a folding chair to reach her Christmas ornaments. Suddenly the chair collapsed. Mrs. Cook heard a voice urging her to "Go with the chair!"

Mrs. Cook did and ended up on the attic floor, bruised, but all right. Had she tried to jump clear of the chair, she might have fallen through the opening in the attic floor. She also might have caught her head in the rope loop, which she had been holding, and hung herself.

As Mrs. Cook sat on the attic floor calming herself, the ghost appeared. He told her, "That is how I died." He hadn't killed himself on purpose—it had been an acci-

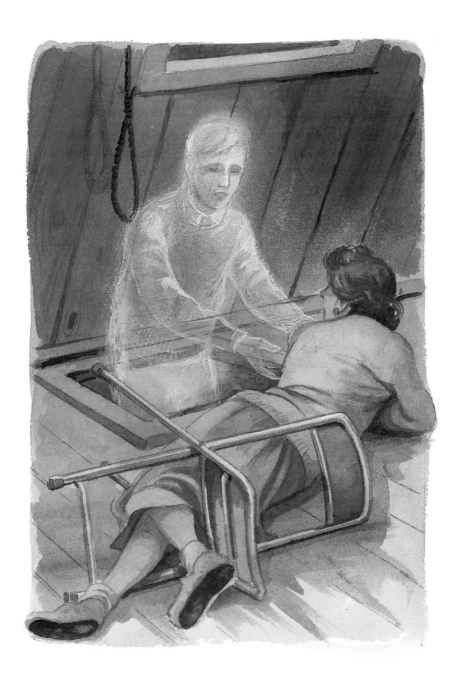

"I just can't figure out why that ghost keeps coming around here."

dent. His mission was to prevent such a tragedy from happening again.

I'm Not Going Until I Finish

If you're living in a haunted house, you may want to try to figure out if your ghost has a reason for haunting you. Those footsteps in the night might be intended to lead you to a murdered body. Those moans and groans might mean, "Pay the butcher." That ghostly figure might be trying to protect you from danger. Whatever the reason for the haunting, you'd better figure it out. Ghosts have been known to stick around hundreds of years, trying to complete their missions.

Chapter 4
Poltergeists

Noisy Spirits

The name poltergeist means "noisy spirit." It is a specific kind of haunting. Most other hauntings consist of footsteps in the night and the occasional sight of a ghostly figure, who may or may not be able to interact with people. Poltergeist hauntings are much more active. They start small. First there are strange raps and knocks. Then small objects are moved or thrown. As the poltergeist gains strength, furniture moves, pools of water appear, and electrical equipment breaks down. Things start to appear and disappear, and fires break out in strange places without any reason. Ghosts are sometimes seen, and sometimes a small ghostly animal as well.

Poltergeist activity usually seems to center on one particular person in a house. This person is called a focal person. The focal person is more likely to be a girl than a boy and is most likely to be someone just entering the teenage years. When that person is nearby, things go crazy. Objects fly around, strange noises are heard, and things burst into flame. When that person leaves, things quiet down. Obviously, investigators always suspect the focal person of faking the haunting. And in about one-third of the cases investigated, it is discovered that someone in the house, often the focal person, has faked the whole thing. But, in the other cases, something genuinely strange seems to be going on.

The Manning Poltergeist

Everything was perfectly normal in the Manning house until one morning in February of 1967. When Mr. Manning came downstairs that morning, he found a valuable silver mug, which normally sat on a display shelf, lying on the living room floor. It was a small incident, soon forgotten—except that a few days later it happened again. No one in the house admitted knowing anything about it.

Without telling anyone, Derek Manning put a powder around the mug to try to figure out how the mug moved. The next morning there were no marks in the powder, the mug was on the floor, and a vase of flowers had been moved.

After that, things began to go crazy in the Manning household. Strange knockings were heard all over the house. All kinds of objects moved when no one in the house could have moved them. Once the young daughter in the family was looking for her eraser. Suddenly it

floated up from the floor where it had dropped and flew through the air, landing next to her.

For three months the family was frightened and confused by these odd events. Then abruptly, the incidents stopped. Later the family learned that the disturbances had probably been caused by a poltergeist.

A Teenage Energy Source

In the Manning family, the strange events seemed to focus on eleven-year-old Matthew. Noises did occur when he wasn't around, but objects stayed in place. He was in the room when his sister's eraser flew through the air. When Matthew stayed at a friend's house for a few days, things were calm. But when he came back, trouble erupted more wildly than before. Matthew did not seem to be deliberately causing things to happen, but there did seem to be an energy he couldn't control coming from him, sort of like electricity. In most poltergeist cases, someone in the house seems to give off an energy force, and something seems to be able to use that energy and cause mischief.

No one knows what it is that taps into that energy. In Matthew's case, perhaps it was Matthew himself—though not on purpose. When Matthew grew up, he seemed to have the power to move objects just by thinking about moving them. Scientists call this ability psychokinesis (si-ko-kuh-NE-sis) or mind over matter. Matthew could have been moving objects without even knowing it before he had that power under control. However, as an adult, Matthew also claimed to be able to communicate with the "spirit world." He would hold a pen over a piece of paper, and the pen would move under the control of "spirits." The spirits sent messages or drew works of art. One spirit even diagnosed illnesses. It could be that the poltergeist activity was caused by those spirits trying to communicate—or just having a little fun. You can read about it in Matthew's book, *The Link*.

Bedroom wrecked by a poltergeist, Cheshire, 1952 (courtesy Fortean Picture Library)

The Manning family suffered flying objects and strange noises for three months. This is typical of most poltergeist hauntings. The poltergeist usually causes trouble for a few weeks or a couple of months and then leaves as suddenly as it came. It also usually never returns to the same house. However, the Mannings suffered another poltergeist attack three years later, the second time even more violently than the first. After months of trouble, during which it looked as if the poltergeist would never leave, Matthew learned he could stop the poltergeist activity by channeling his "energy" into communicating with the spirit world.

In this the Manning family was lucky. Most families suffering from a poltergeist are not so lucky. Usually, nothing anyone does can make a poltergeist quit until it decides to quit.

The Enfield Poltergeist

The "Harper" family had to wait and wait and wait until their poltergeist finally left—almost two years after it arrived.

In 1980 Guy Lyon Playfair described a remarkable poltergeist haunting which happened to the "Harper" family in Enfield, England. He changed the name of the family to protect them, but everything else he recorded in his book, This House is Haunted, he believes to be the absolute truth.

Mrs. Harper and her four children, Rose (age 13), Janet (age 11), Pete (age 10), and Jimmy (age 7), lived in a small two-story, row house in Enfield, England. While putting the children to bed the evening of August 31, 1977, Mrs. Harper heard a strange shuffling noise. Then she heard four loud knocks, and a dresser slid about eighteen inches across the floor. Mrs. Harper pushed the heavy dresser back into place, but it slid out again. She started to push it back again, but this time it wouldn't move. It was as if someone were pushing on it from the other side. Mrs. Harper became frightened and took her children to her next-door neighbor's house. From there she called the police.

Both the neighbors and then the police searched the house. They couldn't find any cause for what had happened, but they, too, heard the strange knockings and then saw a chair slide several feet across a room when no one was near it. The two constables said that the only laws being broken were the laws of nature and that there was nothing they could do. They suggested calling a scientist and left.

Mrs. Harper was able to contact some investigators who were experienced with poltergeist hauntings, but they weren't able to do much for her. The next months were frustrating, annoying, and scary. Marbles, Lego blocks, and stones were hurled round the house constantly. No one could tell where they came from. It looked as if they actually came right through the ceiling. Almost always it was clear that no one in the house could have thrown the objects. And no one got any sleep until well into the night. Loud knocks sounded all over the house. Bedcovers and pillows were snatched from the children's beds, and sometimes the children themselves were

thrown out of beds onto the floors. Then the poltergeist started moving larger objects. The furniture moved around at random. Sometimes heavy couches and chairs overturned while someone was sitting on them. Once a heavy iron fire grate tore itself from the floor and flew across the room.

As time passed, more and more incidents plagued the Harper household. The poltergeist seemed to be showing off all it could do. It tried balancing acts with the furniture, putting chairs on top of cabinets, and then a balancing act with one of the children, moving Janet from her bed to

the top of a large radio set while she was sleeping. Knocking wasn't a fast enough way to communicate, so the poltergeist took over one of the children, usually Janet, and spoke in a harsh, low voice, a voice which Janet could not have made without hurting her throat. The poltergeist would sometimes talk with people for hours, yet Janet's throat was never strained. The voice told the Harpers that he used to live in the house and that he liked to annoy them.

It seemed clear that Janet was the focal person for the poltergeist activity, but time and time again, things happened that neither she nor anyone else could possibly have done. Once Janet claimed that while she was in her room, a mysterious force had caused her to bounce up and down on her bed and then pass through the wall of the bedroom into the house attached to the other side. Even with everything that had already happened, this seemed impossible to believe. Yet a stranger, passing by, saw Janet through her bedroom window, bouncing high in the air, flat on her back. The mattress on her bed didn't have enough spring to allow her to go more than a couple inches, but the man saw her going up and down several feet. Then they checked the room opposite Janet's in the house next door. They found a book on the floor in that room that they knew had been in Janet's room a few minutes before. It was called *Fun and Games for Children*.

But even after that spectacular trick, the poltergeist wasn't done showing off. It continued to throw the children out of bed and move heavy furniture around—often taking just seconds to rearrange an entire room. It bent spoons and a metal teapot lid in the kitchen. It made electrical equipment break. It even started small fires. Like most poltergeist fires, these fires were more annoying than dangerous. They started in unusual places, for no apparent reason, and didn't burn normally. One time a fire started in a closed drawer. It burned several things in the drawer, including the outside of a box of matches. However, the matches in the box did not ignite. Also, like most poltergeist fires, these fires put themselves out before too much damage was done.

In all, thirty different people saw things they couldn't

explain happen in the Harper household. The investigators managed to photograph and tape record some of the events. But no one could figure out what caused them to happen. Finally, though, almost two years after they began, the poltergeist activities slowed down and then stopped. The Harper family had peace and quiet again.

Over and Over Again

Poltergeists have been reported throughout history all over the world. The first written report came from 858 B.C. A family reported that an "evil spirit" was throwing stones and shaking the walls of their house with loud knockings. Down through the years, the same report came over and over again—a convent in France, a minister's house in England, a poor family in Brazil, a rich family in Connecticut all reported a mysterious force disturbing their houses. In fact, somewhere in the world

"There is always a simple, scientific answer for everything."

today, some household is probably suffering with a poltergeist haunting.

Hoax or Haunting?

And suffering is the right word. A person can learn to live with a ghost in the house. You can look the other way and pretend not to see it or try to make friends with it. It's hard to do either of those things when you're being pelted with marbles that seem to have come out of nowhere. Skeptics insist that such tricks have to come from the young people who are almost always present. Believers, though, wonder how young people, without any particular training, could fool parents and investigators for months on end. They also wonder why such young people would always, through three thousand years, choose the same strange activities to annoy their elders. Perhaps scientists will be able to tell us someday—but to do so, they may have to rewrite the laws of nature.

Chapter 5

Animal Ghosts

Animal ghosts are not as common as human ghosts, but they do turn up occasionally. Animals seem to haunt for many of the same reasons people do. Some seem to enjoy causing mischief and annoying people. Many are pets trying to return to their owners. Some seem to have a mission of their own to accomplish, and some seem to have once been human, but are now condemned to an animal form. And some don't seem to fall into any category!

Gef the Gossip

Mr. and Mrs. James T. Irving worked an isolated farm on a small island near Ireland. Their two oldest children had moved away, but their youngest daughter still lived at home.

The Irvings had something else living in their house, too—an uninvited animal ghost named Gef.

The Irvings first heard Gef in September of 1931. Hissing, spitting, and growling sounds came from the attic. It sounded as if there was an animal trapped up there. Mr. Irving searched, but found nothing. He put down poison and stalked whatever it was with a gun, but he never caught anything.

Then one day the noises changed. They went from animal sounds to the sound of a gurgling baby, and then to a pleading bark. Mr. Irving cautiously answered the sounds. He made a number of animal sounds, following each sound with the name of the animal. To his surprise, a shrill, high-pitched voice echoed back not only the animal sounds, but also the animal names. Mr. Irving recited some nursery rhymes. The voice echoed them as well. Mr. Irving didn't know what was haunting his house, but the thing could now talk.

And talk he did. Within weeks, Gef, as he called himself, could speak fluently. In fact, he soon made a pest of himself, asking questions, making weird noises, and throwing objects about. When asked who or what he was, Gef said he was "a ghost in the form of a weasel." Later, he proudly described himself as "a little clever, extra-clever mongoose." And, in fact, the Irvings did occasionally catch sight of a small, furry creature that looked something like a weasel or mongoose.

Gef didn't act much like an ordinary animal or even an ordinary ghost. He spoke in Russian (or at least he told everyone that it was Russian), sang songs in Spanish, and recited poetry in Welsh. He read people's minds and especially enjoyed telling the Irvings all kinds of gossip

about their neighbors. Once Gef described having visited a mansion twenty miles away. The Irvings had never been there, but when a visitor checked Gef's descriptions of the house, he found them to be accurate. Gef had even described some lion decorations on a fireplace which the owner of the house hadn't even known about. The Irvings and different investigators checked a lot of the information Gef gave and found it to be accurate—sometimes to the embarrassment of the Irvings' neighbors.

Many investigators visited the Irvings, but none could explain the things Gef did or knew. Some thought he was a poltergeist. Others thought he was the ghost of an actual animal (which doesn't explain how he could talk). Others, of course, thought he was a hoax. The Irvings weren't scared, but they were annoyed by Gef's antics. Several times they considered moving, and finally, in 1935, they did. After they left, no one saw or heard from Gef again.

Okehampton Castle (courtesy Fortean Picture Library)

The Lady is a Dog

Lady Mary Howard lived in England in the sixteenth century. Among her many crimes, she reportedly poisoned several husbands. You would expect that she wouldn't be able to rest peacefully—and she doesn't.

Every night for the last several hundred years, reports Daniel Cohen in *Ghostly Animals*, Lady Mary Howard has haunted Okehampton Castle. Her ghost appears in the form of a black dog and races beside a coach filled with bones and driven by a headless coachman. She always takes one blade of grass from the lawn of Okehampton Castle, where she once lived, and carries it to another of her old homes. The villagers who live nearby have seen the ghost dog and the coach. They claim that Lady Howard is doomed to repeat this journey every night until every single blade of grass in the huge lawn is removed. Then she will have paid for her crimes and may rest in peace.

Marks made on Blythburgh Church, supposedly by a black dog (courtesy Fortean Picture Library)

Black Dogs

There are hundreds of stories of black-dog ghosts haunting the English countryside—and none of these dogs is up to any good. When a black dog is sighted, it is believed to be a sign that something terrible is going to happen. Villagers fear that these phantom black dogs are demons, and many families believe that if a black dog appears in their house, someone in the family will die in the next year. There are stories of ghost black dogs attacking lonely travelers—and stories of ghost black dogs with supernatural powers.

Ghostly Guides

All in all, ghost dogs have a bad reputation, but in some instances they really don't deserve it. Take, for instance, a case reported by Beth Scott and Michael Norman in *Haunted Heartland.*

One night many years ago, St. Louis, Missouri, lay wrapped in a fierce blizzard. Dr. John J. O'Brien stared out at the driving snow. He was worried about one of his patients, a Mrs. Kilpatrick. She had a bad heart and hadn't been doing well lately. Dr. O'Brien didn't want to go out into the storm, but something seemed to tell him Mrs. Kilpatrick needed him. He had learned to rely on those feelings—they had saved some of his patients' lives in the past—and so now he decided he had to make sure she was all right. There weren't any telephones in those days, so he had to go to her. He hitched his horse to his buggy and headed for Mrs. Kilpatrick's house. His wife watched the lights of his buggy disappear into the snow and then

she prayed that he'd make it safely through the storm.

The roads looked different in the snow than in the daylight. He tried to find his way down a maze of country roads, but Dr. O'Brien simply couldn't see far enough ahead even to be sure he was on a road. He feared that he would never find the Kilpatrick house.

Then, suddenly, Dr. O'Brien heard barking. The sound got louder and louder, and then two huge dogs appeared. They must be the Kilpatrick dogs, he thought. The dogs guided him through the storm. Left . . . right . . . this way

and that. Finally, Dr. O'Brien saw a light coming from a window. It was the Kilpatrick house!

Mrs. Kilpatrick's anxious husband greeted the doctor with relief. Mrs. Kilpatrick was having trouble breathing. The doctor tended her and then stayed a few minutes to talk to Mr. Kilpatrick. Dr. O'Brien told him of how the dogs had guided him to the house.

"But I have no dogs," said Mr. Kilpatrick, amazed.

It seems that in a late-night, winter storm, two ghost dogs appeared to guide a doctor safely to his patient.

Returning Pets

Most stories of animal ghosts are not quite so dramatic. But if you had lost a pet, you might think that the best animal ghost would be a pet that returned to its owner—or you might think that would be just as spooky as any other ghost.

When Mrs. Marie C. Demler went into the hospital to have a baby, she left her beloved dog Mac with some friends. One night in the hospital, Mrs. Demler was shocked to see Mac come into her room. She greeted him happily and petted him as he nuzzled her hand. But as soon as she touched him, she noticed that Mac was sopping wet. At that moment the dog vanished. Mrs. Demler learned later that Mac had drowned at just that same time.

Mrs. Demler was glad her dog had been able to say good-bye, but in *Animal Ghosts* Raymond Bayless tells of a family that didn't find the return of their pet to be such a comfort.

When Red, a beautiful Irish setter, died August 27, 1965, the Baterski family missed him greatly. He had been part of the family for fourteen years. Then, three nights after the dog had been buried, the Baterskis were haunted by a strange barking. They knew right away that it was Red. For fourteen years they had heard Red's unusual bark. It sounded like a "hoarse seal." But now Red was dead. How could this be?

After hearing the bark for several weeks, Mrs. Baterski insisted that they dig up Red's grave to be sure he was dead. Of course, he was. Finally, the Baterskis got a new

"Stay!"

dog, a little German shepherd puppy. Then, the barking stopped.

Animals in the Spirit World

Animal ghosts seem to be able to take on as many different roles as human ghosts. They can cause mischief or bring terror, comfort the lonely or fulfill a mission. It might be just wishful thinking that conjures them up, but no doubt some people find comfort in the thought that animals, too, have an existence in the spirit world.

Chapter 6

Vengeful Ghosts

It would be nice to think that only loving, caring ghosts haunt the living. But, in fact, revenge also seems to be a strong enough motive to cause a ghost to stick around.

The Muir Curse

In the early 1800's Howard Thornton Muir, a wealthy Virginian, moved to Missouri and built a beautiful mansion. For many years he and his family lived in luxury and entertained their friends lavishly. Then tragedy struck. In *Haunted Heartland* Beth Scott and Michael Norman tell of the death of Muir's young daughter, Nancy.

One morning Nancy awoke with a mysterious fever. She had never been sick before. Her father summoned the best doctors, but they could do nothing. The young girl grew weaker and weaker and finally died.

Howard Muir brooded over the loss of his daughter until he went a little crazy. Nancy had never been ill before, he thought. Why should she have died so suddenly? Somebody must have caused her to die.

His thoughts went to his slaves, living in miserable shacks out behind his great mansion. Was there one who had wished his daughter ill? Yes—old Aunt Eternity. Nancy had once caught Aunt Eternity stealing a silk scarf.

In his crazed mind, Howard Muir felt he needed no proof. He grabbed a whip and headed for Aunt Eternity's hut. As Aunt Eternity lay dying on the floor, she screamed out a curse upon the entire Muir family.

Aunt Eternity's curse worked. Within a few years the Muirs lost all their money, and every member of the family died suddenly. No one ever lived again in the beautiful mansion, and it fell into ruins. You can still see those ruins today—and might also see a ghost which the neighbors report haunts the old mansion, wandering aimlessly through the empty rooms.

The Ghost in the Well

Warren Armstrong tells of a vengeful ghost in his book, *The Authentic Shudder*.

Peggy was a maid in a large household. One day she had a fierce fight with her employer. Peggy wouldn't stop yelling, so finally her employer sent her out to get some water at the well. As Peggy left, still grumbling, her employer wished Peggy might "fall and break her neck on the way." And Peggy did. She slipped on some ice and fell into the well, breaking her neck.

Peggy's employer was to regret her hasty words for the rest of her life. Peggy's ghost began haunting the manor house and grounds. She would pop out of the well or send bloodcurdling screams echoing through the hallways. Lovers might be terrified by the touch of icy fingers on their necks. And even though Peggy's employer has since died, neighbors report that Peggy is haunting still.

The Bell Witch

Another ghost that was impossible to get rid of was known as The Bell Witch.

In the early 1800's John and Lucy Bell owned a small farm in Tennessee. They had four sons and a daughter, Betsy. One evening in 1817 the family heard strange knocking sounds in their house. At first Mr. Bell thought it was just the children. But the noises continued, night after night. And they grew stranger and stranger; strangling, choking, gurgling, and sighing sounds haunted the family.

Then something began tormenting twelve-year-old Betsy. Though no one was near her, there would suddenly be the sound of a slap, and Betsy's cheek would turn red. She was also pinched viciously and her hair was pulled.

Next, objects began flying about the house. And then, the ghost developed a voice. A woman's voice told the family that she was the spirit of old Kate Batts. She had come back to get revenge on John Bell and his family because, she claimed, John Bell had cheated her in a business deal. Word spread of the cruel pranks the ghost played on the family, and people began calling the ghost the Bell Witch.

For almost four years, the Bell Witch tormented the Bells, especially John and Betsy. When Betsy became engaged to a young man, the witch pleaded with her to break the engagement. When Betsy wouldn't, the ghost witch pinched and slapped and yelled at Betsy until Betsy finally gave in.

John Bell suffered even more. His mouth and tongue swelled so much that he sometimes couldn't eat or talk for days. Pain racked his body. The witch just laughed and cursed at him. Soon Bell's health grew so poor that he had to stay in bed. But even then the Bell Witch would not leave him alone. She punched him and hit him and sent him into such terrible fits that his shoes would fly off his feet.

Finally, one night in December of 1820, John Bell's family found him in a coma. In the medicine chest his bottle of medicine was gone, replaced by an almost empty vial of poison. The witch shouted, "It's useless for you to try to revive Old Jack. I've got him this time. He will never get up from that bed again!" At John Bell's funeral, the witch sang songs of victory.

After John Bell's death, the Bell Witch left the family alone for a while. However, some members of that family have reported that to this day, she still occasionally drops in, causing trouble.

Amityville

Sometimes all a person has to do in order to be haunted by a vengeful ghost is to move into the wrong house.

George and Kathy Lutz thought their dream had come true when they moved into 112 Ocean Avenue in Amityville, New York, in December of 1975. The house was big and beautiful with an upstairs playroom for the children, a boathouse, and a swimming pool. But their dream became a terrible nightmare. The house, it seemed, didn't want them.

Strange things began to happen soon after the Lutz family moved into the house. In *The Amityville Horror* Jay

Anson describes how windows opened in the middle of the night, green slime oozed from the walls, and thousands of flies appeared. There were terrible smells and mysterious sounds. One night it sounded as if a marching band was practicing in the living room. Nightmares troubled everyone's sleep, and a huge ghost pig made "friends" with the Lutz's young daughter.

The priest who came to bless the house heard a masculine voice tell him to, "Get out!" as he flicked holy water in the entrance. Afterward the priest suffered an unexplainable illness and several strange accidents. He called George Lutz and tried to tell him to leave the house, but static clouded the phone line, and he was forced to hang up. When he tried again, he could hear the phone ring, but no one answered.

For several weeks the Lutz family tried to tell themselves that the evil presence they felt was just their imagination. George thought his short temper just came from the stress of buying a new house. Kathy noticed that he wasn't taking care of himself and that he always seemed to be cold, but she, too, thought it was just stress. She felt a ghostly presence touch her in the kitchen, and the children refused to play in the upstairs playroom. It was too cold up there despite the fact that the radiator was working perfectly. Gradually the strange incidents occurred more and more frequently. Then one night, the furniture moved violently in the children's room, and the children screamed that a monster without a face was trying to grab them. The Lutz family had had it. In the middle of the night, only twenty-eight days after moving in, they fled from their dream house.

Many people have tried to figure out what happened in Amityville. Some link it to the previous residents. The teenage son of the previous owners suddenly shot to death his entire family one night in that house. Was some of his evil presence still in the house, or had the evil been there before, influencing him to commit his terrible deed? Researchers have learned that the house was built over an Indian burial ground. Some say it may be that their spirits object to their graves being disturbed.

The Lutz family didn't have any of the answers. They just knew they had to escape. They moved across the

"I said I was sorry that I wrecked your bike thirty years ago!"

country to California to flee from the evil that they believed lived in that haunted house.

No Grudges!

Of the many stories about haunted houses, only a few involve vengeful ghosts. But these terrible creatures can certainly make life miserable for the living. So, just to be on the safe side, don't give anyone a reason to hold a grudge against you!

Chapter 7

Is It All Real?

Evidence?

Stories about ghosts and haunted houses are everywhere. For most people these ghost stories are just fun—tales to be told to send a chill up someone's back when the lights are dim. They don't think any ghost story can be taken seriously. But there are people who believe at least some of the stories are real. They think there have been too many strange things reported by sensible, down-to-earth people for every ghost story to be dismissed as just imagination or as some kind of mistake—especially when the stories are backed up with evidence. Even the most skeptical person has to think twice when a ghost is caught on camera.

Newby Church

The Reverend K.F. Lord didn't see anything unusual when he took a picture of the altar in his church one day in the early 1960's. The church at Newby in North Yorkshire did not have a reputation for being haunted. Reverend Lord didn't feel any sudden chills as he took pictures of the church interior where he was the vicar.

When the pictures were developed, though, Reverend Lord got a shock. A very tall, ghostly figure stood on the steps before the altar! Reverend Lord did not have any explanation for how the figure got into his picture. Experts have not found any evidence that the photo was faked. And people who know Reverend Lord are sure he wouldn't deliberately create such a hoax. So, where did that ghostly figure come from?

Newby Church photograph (courtesy Fortean Picture Library)

The Brown Lady of Raynham Hall

At Raynham Hall in Norfolk, England, stories have been told for two centuries about a lady in brown who haunts that large estate. No one knows who she is—or was—but many people have seen her wandering the halls of the mansion and entering a particular room. The ghost is proud and elegant, with her hair neatly done. However, people who have seen her up close report that she has no eyes—just empty sockets! Once a guest, scared by her appearance, shot the lady point blank. But the bullets passed right through her and the lady just continued on her way.

The story of the Brown Lady of Raynham Hall is not an unusual story. This same kind of ghost story is told about hundreds of old houses, especially in England. But, in 1936, two photographers got some evidence that the Brown Lady of Raynham is more than just another ghost story.

On September 19, 1936, two photographers, Indre Shira and Captain Provand, arrived at Raynham Hall. They had been hired by Lady Townshend, the owner of the estate, to photograph the mansion and the grounds.

At 4:00 in the afternoon the two photographers were set up to photograph the main staircase. They took one picture and set up for another. Suddenly, Shira saw something shimmer on the staircase. He shouted, "Quick! Quick! There's something! Are you ready?"

Provand didn't know what Shira was shouting about, but he took the picture. When Shira told him he'd seen a ghost on the stairs, Provand didn't believe him.

The two men argued all the way back to London about whether there had really been a ghost on the stairs. When they developed the negative, Provand caught his breath. There was something there!

The two men quickly called in another man who could testify that they hadn't done anything to the negative. When the picture came out of the developer, they could all clearly see that the shadowy form of a hooded woman stood on the stairs—they had a photograph of the Brown Lady of Raynham Hall!

The photograph of the Brown Lady of Raynham Hall is one of the most famous pictures of a ghost. It and other pictures, such as the one taken at Newby Church, have been hard for skeptics to explain.

The Brown Lady of Raynham Hall (courtesy of Fortean Picture Library)

"Come on, Sarah. This time all I want is the staircase."

Not Proof

But as much as some people would like to believe otherwise, photographs are not proof of the existence of ghosts. It's just too easy for someone to fake a picture or make a mistake about what they are seeing. Experts say there is a chance that the Brown Lady of Raynham Hall is just some unintended trick of the light. And even if the experts can't tell how, the Newby Church photograph could be a hoax. But photographs can't be completely ignored, either. Even if these two photos are not of genuine ghosts, other photographs exist which may be.

Scientific Investigation

Scientific proof is hard to come by. Ghosts are reluctant to pop into a laboratory to undergo tests. (And who can blame them!) Yet, scientists want to be able to measure something before they'll admit it's real. They want there to be rules governing ghostly appearances and a scientific explanation for how ghosts behave. It may be unrealistic to expect the supernatural to follow the laws of nature, but scientists don't know any other way to approach a problem.

Some scientists have investigated haunted houses. They have not learned much. No matter how often a ghost has popped in some place, as soon as an objective reporter pays it a visit, it's nowhere to be seen. Perhaps that's because ghosts don't want anyone investigating them. Or perhaps it's because there are no ghosts.

Scientists have found one puzzling thing in some haunted houses. Frequently they find places in the house that are colder than the rest of the house. The chill doesn't seem to be caused by air-flow problems or any other natural explanation. Still, that doesn't prove that those cold spots are caused by ghosts.

Poltergeist investigators have had more success in their research than investigators of more conventional hauntings. Perhaps that is because there is so much activity associated with poltergeist hauntings. These investigators have been able to tape record the strange knocking sounds and the occasional ghostly voice. They have photographed objects flying about and have sometimes photographed ghosts themselves. But none of these tapes or photographs is clear enough to be proof that only a ghost could be responsible. These investigators have seen enough to know that something is going on, but they aren't able to say for sure just what that something is.

What to Believe?

What then should we believe about all these stories of ghosts and haunted houses? Are they true or are they just stories?

Well, certainly, some of them are just stories. There are always people who pretend to see ghosts. They might think they can make money with their story. They might want their picture in the paper. Or they might just think it's fun to fool people.

And certainly some of the stories are just imagination. It's easy for someone to make a mistake about something he's seen. Late at night, a mouse scurrying about in the attic or the wind moaning past a window can sound like a ghostly visitor. And a shadow on the wall or the gleam of headlights from a passing car can produce a scary specter for anyone who's feeling a little nervous.

But some of these stories can't be dismissed as just imagination. Imagination doesn't make objects fly around a room in broad daylight or cause lights to turn on and off for a whole neighborhood to see. A human figure seen up close can't be dismissed as just a trick of the light.

A Great Mystery

And some of these stories can't be dismissed as hoaxes either. The people telling these stories are careful observers with spotless reputations. They have nothing to gain from telling their incredible stories—in fact, they are likely to be made fun of. They are just as confused and scared about what they've seen as you would be.

So, if the people who report that their houses are

haunted are not deliberately lying and they are not imagining what they've seen, something real must have happened to them. Is there some logical explanation that they just haven't found? Or could it be that there are real ghosts haunting those houses?

Until we are able to answer those questions, haunted houses will remain a Great Mystery!

INDEX